Robert Peary
and Matthew Henson

Betty Lou Kratoville

High Noon Books

ORDER DIRECTLY FROM
ANN ARBOR PUBLISHERS LTD.
P.O. BOX 1, BELFORD
NORTHUMBERLAND NE70 7JX
TEL. 01668 214460 FAX 01668 214484
www.annarbor.co.uk

International Standard Book Number: 1-57128-232-7

10 09 08 07 06 05 04 03 02 01
 0   9   8   7   6   5   4   3   2   1

You'll enjoy all the High Noon Books. Write for
our catalog that lists and describes titles.

Contents

Chapter 1

First Trip

Robert Edwin Peary was born to be an explorer! He was brave. He was stubborn. He was tough. He was headstrong – and he was smart!

He did not start out that way. His father died in 1858 when Peary was only two years old. His mother took the little boy back to Maine to be near her family. All her thoughts seem to fix on her only son. Friends said that Mrs. Peary gave him anything he wanted. They all felt he was a spoiled, difficult child. But she did lead him to the right books and the right hobbies. And she did teach him to be honest and to set high goals for himself.

After public schools in Portland, Peary went to Bowdoin College in Brunswick, Maine.

He studied to become a civil engineer. He also had a lively interest in natural science. For a year he worked as a surveyor in a small town in Maine. Then he moved to Washington, D.C. No one knows why but he joined the navy there.

A few years later the navy sent him to Nicaragua in South America. His job was to map out a route for a canal. It was good training for an explorer. He had to hack his way through swamps and jungles. He waded through water that was knee deep, sometimes up to his waist or neck. After a while, plans for the canal fell through. (Much later it was built through Panama.)

One day after he got back to Washington, Peary wandered into a book store. There he happened to find a book about the amazing Greenland Ice Cap. He read that this dome of ice covers three-fourths of Greenland. It starts a few miles inland from the coast. In some spots it is 8,000 feet thick. At that time, little was known about Greenland or its Ice Cap.

Peary read everything about Greenland he

could get his hands on. There was not a lot to read. No one had yet explored it. But the more he read, the more excited he became. He badly wanted to see that Ice Cap for himself. But how to do it? Could it be crossed on foot or on skis? Would one need a sledge pulled by dogs? First, one had to get to Greenland, not an easy thing to do.

One day he heard about a whaler, the *Eagle*. It was headed to the Arctic whaling grounds off the coast of Greenland. Peary got in touch with the captain. Would he take a passenger? Yes – for $500. At that time Peary was earning only $100 a month in the navy. $500 was a huge sum to him. He went to his mother and borrowed $500. Then he talked the navy into giving him a six-month leave of absence. In May 1886 he left on his first trip to the frozen north.

At that time Greenland belonged to Denmark. (In fact, it still does.) Peary got off the *Eagle* at Godhavn. This was a Danish trading station on the west coast of Greenland.

Peary wanted to find a boat to take him to Ritenbenk, a town next to the western wall of the Ice Cap. Buying a boat was not easy. Peary spoke no Danish. Few people there spoke English. After a while, he was able to get not only a boat but a young Dane to guide him.

In those days there were few maps of Greenland, and they could not be relied on. No matter! Peary and his guide sailed the boat up an inlet to the Ice Cap. Then they started to walk overland. By the end of June they had reached the top of the Ice Cap. The worst part of their trip lay ahead. They kept heading east, dragging two heavy sledges. A wild storm kept them pinned down in their tent for days. After it passed, they pushed on.

The Arctic sun was bright. Some days it melted the Ice Cap beneath them. They had to struggle through waist-deep icy slush. Now and then they had to climb slippery hills.

Then there came a day when their food supply ran low. They had come 120 miles. They were 7,525 feet above sea level. There was nothing to do but return to Godhavn.

No one had gone this far across Greenland before. It caused a mild flurry of interest. It was the first time Peary's name appeared in American newspapers. It certainly would not be the last! When people learned about his Greenland journey, they thought it was just a passing interest. Such a man would surely want to explore other parts of the world. Peary's friends knew better.

His interest in the Arctic dated from his school days. That is the reason he was spellbound by the book he had found about Greenland. Even before he had seen his first iceberg, Peary began to think about reaching the North Pole. He felt he knew the mistakes others had made in trying for the Pole. The British had tried more than once. They had gone in large groups. Peary thought small groups would be better. The British did not use Eskimos. Peary felt that help from Eskimos would be vital.

Peary had learned a lot on his first Ice Cap trip. Most of all he had learned how much he did not know.

He was sure that one day he would return to Greenland. The sooner, the better! Next time he would be sure to pack enough supplies. He would ask a group of Eskimos to go with him. These were the people who really knew the frozen land to the north. Did they know how far north Greenland extended? Did it reach to the North Pole? Peary vowed that one day he would answer these questions. He knew he was not the only one who was planning to explore Arctic lands. Already he thought of it as a race. He would settle for nothing less than being the first man to reach the North Pole.

His leave of absence was up. He had to report back to the navy. He was sent to the Brooklyn Navy Yard. About this time Peary got married. His new wife's name was Josephine. She was just as eager as Peary for him to reach his goal.

One day Peary heard some shocking news. An explorer from Norway had skied all the way across Greenland's Ice Cap. At first Peary was downhearted. He had hoped to be the first. But then he cheered up. After all, the man from Norway had skied across the narrow southern end of Greenland. He, Peary, would cross at the wider northern end. Also, he would try to reach the very northern limits of Greenland.

Now it was time to get to work to raise money for the next trip. It would not be easy but somehow he would do it.

Chapter 2

Second Trip

More than two years passed before Peary could raise the $10,000 he needed for his next journey. He also had to talk the navy into giving him another leave of absence.

He was not alone when he boarded the steamer *Kite* in 1891 for the second trip north. His wife Josephine was with him. She was eager to go. Peary was eager to have her with him. Also in the group was the African-American, Matthew Henson.

Henson was ten years younger than Peary. He had been born in Maryland. He ran away from home at age 11 after both parents had died. A year later he went to sea as a cabin boy. He was working in a hat store in Washington, D.C.

when he met Peary. Peary knew a good man when he saw one! He hired Henson at once as an aide. From then on Henson went with Peary on all of his trips. Through the years they became good friends. Peary knew he could rely on Henson's strength and courage in times of danger.

Also in the group were Dr. Frederick Cook (of whom we will hear much later); Eivind Astrup from Norway; Langdon Gibson, who was an expert on birds; and a young daredevil, John Verhoeff. Verhoeff was a troublemaker. He hated rules, even those made for the good of the group. And he had a hot temper. One day he went looking for minerals and was never seen again. Peary did not get along well with either Astrup or Cook.

At first all went well on board the *Kite*. Then Peary broke his leg in a freak accident. He was strolling on the deck of the *Kite*. A huge chunk of falling ice struck the ship's rudder. It, in turn, spun the wheel out of the steersman's hands. This caused the tiller to smash into

Peary. It broke his leg. They docked in Inglefield Gulf near Greenland's northwest corner. Peary had to be carried ashore. They made camp, and here Peary began his important Eskimo friendships.

During the winter he was laid up with his leg bound tightly to a board. It gave him time to talk to the people of the North and to learn from them. They showed him how to drive a dog sled and how to build an igloo.

He learned the right clothes to wear in sub zero weather. He learned how important it was on a trip to store enough fresh meat to guard against scurvy.

At this time he wrote about the Eskimos to a friend:

These people are trustworthy and hardy. They will yet prove their value to mankind. With their help the world will discover the North Pole.

Peary was right on all counts!

By spring Peary's leg had healed. He felt

strong and fit. It was time to set out on a 700-mile trek. On this trip Peary tried for the first time the methods he would later use to reach the North Pole. He traveled on skis. Eskimo dogs pulled supply sledges.

In July he reached the northeastern shores of Greenland. He still did not know how much farther north the land went. The group feasted on musk oxen to gain strength. Then it was time to start the long hard trip back to base camp.

By the end of August the expedition was on its way home. Back in New York, the welcome was a warm one. Peary was becoming famous. He was not a humble man so he didn't mind the fame at all.

At once Peary threw himself into raising money for a third trip. In 103 days he gave 105 lectures and earned $20,000. Henson often went with him. He wore Eskimo furs and took Eskimo huskies along. This added a lot of color to Peary's talks and helped to raise money. Funds also came from science clubs and from men who wished they could join the expedition but were bound by duties at home.

Now the only snag was the navy. It had other plans for Peary. What to do? He got in touch with some important people he knew. They got in touch with the navy. Result: Peary got a three-year leave of absence. The last problem had been solved. It was time to go.

Chapter 3

Third Trip

Once again Josephine Peary was at her husband's side when the steamer *Falcon* left New York heading north. This time she gave the group a bit of excitement. On September 12, 1893, the Pearys' daughter was born. She was the first American child to begin life in the Arctic Circle.

In a sense, little Marie Peary's birth was one of the few happy events of the third trip. It seemed as if anything that could go wrong *did* go wrong. Twice Peary and his men set out across the Ice Cap. Twice blizzards forced them back. An iceberg split in two. This caused great waves that swamped vital fuel supplies at base camp. Some of the dogs grew sick and died.

Lieutenant Peary's Arctic Steamer "Falcon"

Peary had brought along mules and homing pigeons to try in the frigid weather. They, too, sickened and died.

When a boat left for home, everyone wanted to go with it. Even Josephine, her baby, and the child's nurse chose to go. Left behind were Peary, Henson, and one other man, Hugh Lee. These three men tried one more long trip and almost starved to death. They lost all their dogs but one.

This expedition did have one deed to point to with pride. About 75 years earlier, an English explorer had found three huge meteorites that had fallen from space. They were on an island off the coast of Greenland. The Eskimos had given them names. One looked like a sleeping animal, so they called it the "Dog." Another was known as the "Woman." A third, the largest, was called the "Tent."

For years the Eskimos had made tools from the metal in the giant meteorites. Once Americans came to their shores, they had a better source for tools. So they didn't mind when Peary decided to take the meteorites back to the United States. The ship was large enough for only the Dog and the Woman. Much later they both were placed in the American Museum of Natural History. The Tent ended up in the Brooklyn Navy Yard after many years.

Some people thought the 1893-1895 trip had been a failure. Peary did not agree. He felt he had learned a lot. He knew Henson had learned a lot, too.

The Arctic was in his head and heart now. All his energies would be spent on when and how he could reach the North Pole.

Chapter 4

Try, Try Again

Peary's efforts to get ready for another Arctic trip ran into trouble right away. The navy was getting tired of his being away from his duties so much of the time. One day in April he received new orders. He was to report for duty at a naval station in San Francisco.

San Francisco! Peary was shocked. He did not want to go to California. He wanted to go back to Greenland. He wrote at once to the head of the navy. He asked for another leave of absence. He was turned down. Sadly he packed his bags and was ready to leave for San Francisco. Just about that time he happened to meet a man from New York. This man was a friend of President McKinley.

"How much time do you need?" the man asked.

"Five years," said Peary. He did not have much hope. But, wonder of wonders, this time his request for a leave of absence was quickly granted. Five years!

Between 1898 and 1902 Peary made several trips to survey Greenland and nearby islands. Many times he and his team lived under terrible conditions. On one of his tramps across snowfields, his feet were frostbitten. The toes on both feet were badly frozen. A doctor in the group amputated eight toes. (The other two toes were amputated later when Peary returned to the States.)

Would he be able to walk? The doctor said no. Peary said yes! Yet for a time he could travel only by lashing himself to a sledge. His Eskimo friends drove the sledge pulled by huskies.

Peary learned a lot on these trips. In May he and his group rounded the tip of Greenland. At last he knew exactly how far north

Greenland extended. This was knowledge the world had not yet had. It meant new maps could be drawn. Maps that were now correct.

More than once during these years Peary tried to reach the North Pole. More than once foul weather forced him to turn back. Once he was within 343 miles of his goal. But supplies ran short, and the weary men had to return to base camp. Everyone wondered how Peary kept going. He was in great pain as his injured feet bumped over the rough ice. Yet he never complained.

To add to his troubles, bad news came from home. Josephine wrote sadly that their second daughter had died. Not too much later, Peary learned that his beloved mother had also died. It seemed hard to know that he would never see his daughter or mother again. These were bitter blows to a man far away in a strange cold land.

No one blamed Peary for feeling low. For a short time he wondered if his goal could ever be reached. It was the only time he had any real doubts. He wrote, "My dream of sixteen years is ended. I close the book and turn to other things. They will not be as interesting. But they will be better suited to my years." He was then 45 years old.

His gloom did not last long. He was ready to go on no matter what it took. But he knew his men were tired and ready to give up. It was time to go home to rest and to make plans for a final try at the North Pole.

Chapter 5

The Ice Breaker

By this time Peary was certain of one thing. If men and dogs were ever to reach the North Pole, part of the journey would have to be made by ship. Not just any ship. A strong ship with powerful engines. An ice breaker!

Where to find such a ship? How to pay for it? Peary didn't know where to turn. Then a group of men who believed in him handed him a check for $100,000. It was a huge sum of money in those days. Today that $100,000 would most likely be worth more than a million dollars. So Peary was able to have his ship built. He named it the *Roosevelt* after Theodore Roosevelt, who was now President of the United States. The two men were good friends.

They were alike in many ways.

In some places the sides of the *Roosevelt* were 30 inches thick. The body of the ship was braced with iron and heavy timbers. Part of its bow was covered with steel. Would it be able to break its way through 350 miles of almost solid ice? Peary was not sure. Only time would tell.

Five other explorers had joined Peary and Henson on this expedition. The *Roosevelt* had a crew of 22 men to run the ship. And then there were the Eskimos. When the ship reached Greenland, 40 Eskimo men, women, and children came on board. Some of the Eskimo men would go with Peary and his group on the last stages of their journey to the Pole. Henson would choose the Eskimos who were to make that journey. Over the years the Eskimos had grown to love and respect him. He spoke their language better than Peary or any of the other American explorers.

Mile after mile the *Roosevelt* rammed and pushed through the thick ice. In September the ship reached Cape Sheridan. This was a small

The ship was blocked by ice.

village on Ellesmere Island. Ellesmere Island was due west of Greenland.

Heavy fog often swirled around the ship. It hid the sea from sight. Now and then the ship would hit a large mass of floating ice. Then it would pitch and shudder and shake. There would be a loud crash. Men would look at each other in fear. Never had they been in such a place before!

Somehow the *Roosevelt* broke through the ice and went on. Peary was sure the ship could stand even heavier blows than it had run up against so far. After all he had watched every inch of it being built. Most of the ideas to turn it into an ice breaker were his. He and Henson often stood on deck when the fog lifted to watch the sturdy little vessel make its way through the dangerous frozen sea.

Two miles beyond Cape Sheridan the ship finally was blocked by solid ice. It could go no farther north. Back to Cape Sheridan for the long, dark winter. Soon the ice that pressed tightly around the ship was frozen solid. The men lived on the *Roosevelt* for five months.

They had their work cut out for them. During the dark winter days they moved thousands of pounds of food and supplies to Cape Columbia. This cape was about 93 miles to the northwest. The men built igloos there out of blocks of snow. They stored the food and supplies they had brought from the ship in the igloos. Peary planned to use this small camp as a base. From it he would travel across the ice and snow to the North Pole.

By now Peary had learned that he must have a careful plan for the long journey northward. He knew this plan must be perfect in every detail. One mistake would mean failure and even death.

On a map the North Pole can be seen to be in the middle of the Arctic Ocean. This ocean is covered with ice the year round. It never melts. It was clear that Peary and his men would have to walk nearly 500 miles over jagged ice to reach the North Pole. Then they would have to turn around and head back to their base camp. If they ran out of food or became too tired, they would fail. Peary made sure that every man understood every detail of his plan.

Peary divided the men into seven groups. They would all follow the same trail. But they would travel separately. The lead group would break a trail through the ice and snow. When these men grew too tired to go on, another group would take the lead. Peary and the men in his group would always be last. He knew they must save their strength for the final part of the dangerous journey.

As they kept hiking northward, one group after another would be sent back to base camp at Cape Columbia. Peary, Henson, and their group would then go on alone. By this time, there would only be enough food left for a few men to reach the Pole.

This then was the plan. Peary could hardly wait for winter to be over and the darkness to end.

Chapter 6

The North Pole

Near the end of January, Peary saw a faint glow appear in the southern sky. The long Arctic night was ending. It was time to begin the northward expedition.

The main journey began at Cape Columbia on February 28, 1909. The lead party was under the command of Bob Bartlett. It was his job to break a trail for groups coming behind. The second group left a few hours later. It was led by George Borup. His task was to store supplies three days out on the trail and then return for a second load of supplies. The five other groups left the next day. Henson was leading. Peary brought up the rear. A freezing east wind was blowing. It numbed their faces as they walked behind the heavy sledges.

They made about 10 miles the first day. That night they slept in two igloos built by men in the lead groups. They had 400 miles to go.

Even the best plans cannot cover all chance events. Peary was soon faced with a major problem — a fuel shortage. The rough ice had jolted some of the sledges. When they tipped this way and that, damage to the cans of fuel had caused them to leak.

Borup was already on the way back to base camp for supplies. He had to be found to be told to bring extra fuel. Another group leader, Ross Marvyn, went after him. He caught up with Borup just as he was starting back with the new supplies. Borup added cans of fuel to the loaded sledges.

Then the weather changed. It became much warmer. Patches of water opened up. Borup and Marvyn had to wait five days before starting out. They came close to missing Peary on the trail. Somehow they managed to find him.

Weeks went by. One group after another

turned back to Camp Columbia as planned. By the end of March all the groups had turned back except Bob Bartlett's and Peary's (with Henson). They were making 15 or 16 miles a day.

One night they were all camping together. The ice floe they were on began to break up. Peary and Henson quickly got their teams across a wide gap of water to safety. Bartlett was left stranded on a small floe. Luckily, his floe drifted near the edge where Peary and Henson were waiting. As the two floes came together for a few seconds, Bartlett's team scrambled across.

Now it was time for Bartlett's group to turn back. Only Peary and Henson's group was left. It was up to them to make the final stages of the journey. With them were four Eskimos and 40 dogs. The Eskimos were named Ootah, Edgingwah, Ooqueah, and Seegloo. They were still about 130 miles from the Pole.

Onward they stumbled. The frozen ridges of ice and snow seemed never to end. At ten

All of the groups except two had turned back.

o'clock on the morning of April 6, 1909, they knew they were close. Only a few miles lay between them and the North Pole. Peary's dream was about to come true. Yet the past weeks had taken their toll. He was now 52 years old. He had crippled painful feet. He was simply too tired to go on. He had to stop to rest. After a few hours of sleep, he awoke. He wrote in his diary,

> *The Pole at last. I cannot bring*
> *myself to believe it.*

That evening Peary, Henson, and the Eskimos hiked the last few miles across the ice. Peary checked and rechecked his compass with great care. He had to be sure he was at the Pole. There could be no doubt.

The men proudly raised the flag of the United States at the top of the world.

The weather was fine so they stayed at the North Pole for 30 hours. Then they began the long trip southward. They made the return trip with a speed that was hard to believe. On April 23 they reached the camp at Cape Columbia.

They were given a warm welcome from the men who had returned before them. Peary wrote in his diary,

My life's work is accomplished!

The Americans, Robert Peary and Matthew Henson, had done what other men had been trying to do for nearly 400 years!

Chapter 7

The Lie!

On his way home Peary met two Eskimos with a strange tale. They told him that they had traveled with Dr. Frederick Cook. Cook had ordered them to say that they had covered many miles over sea ice. The truth was that they had never been out of sight of land. Peary remembered Cook from the time that Cook had been a member of one of Peary's early Greenland trips. The Eskimos' story puzzled Peary. But it didn't worry him.

He and Henson stopped at Labrador on their way home. From there he sent off his famous message:

"Stars and Stripes nailed to the Pole!"
While in Labrador, he and Henson went on a

walrus hunt. Peary wanted to be sure that his Eskimo friends had enough meat for the winter.

When at last Peary reached home, he could not believe his ears! Dr. Cook was claiming that he had reached the North Pole in April 1908. This would place him at the Pole a full year before Peary. Even worse, people believed him. Cook was a national hero!

In a fury, Peary sent off a flurry of telegrams to American newspapers. In these telegrams he called Cook a fraud and a liar. This started a huge argument. Everyone took sides. Most Americans seemed to believe Cook. He was a pleasant fellow, easy to like. Peary, on the other hand, tended to speak frankly. This often offended people.

One newspaper decided to take a poll. Who had reached the Pole first – Cook or Peary? The results of the poll were shocking. Cook got 73,239 votes. Peary got only 2,814. Even worse, many people thought Peary had not reached the Pole at all.

Peary set out to prove his case with facts

and figures. He had kept good records. They showed clearly that his final camp was just two miles from the Pole. He had walked north for those two miles. Then his compass showed he was walking south. In all he took 13 different readings of the position of the sun. He took them from four different directions. He took them at four different times. He wrote, "I had passed over or very near the point where north and south and east and west blend into one."

Peary might not have been believed by his own countrymen. But people outside the United States believed him. Scientific groups all over the world accepted his claim. They did not believe Cook.

As a further insult, Peary was called to testify before Congress. He was forced to answer questions that were both stupid and unfriendly. The public stayed against Peary for a long time. Things might have stayed that way but for one bit of luck. Good luck for Peary. Bad luck for Cook. Cook was arrested for an oil stock fraud. A jury convicted him. He was sentenced to 14 years in prison. Now people began to wonder about Cook. If he had lied about the oil deal, maybe he had lied about the North Pole, too.

The whole matter was summed up by one writer who said, "Cook was a liar and a gentleman. Peary was neither."

Josephine Peary always thought that the scandal had shortened her husband's life.

Chapter 8

After the Pole

Everyone should have a hideaway! A quiet place where one can find peace and enjoy life and family. Robert Peary believed this. He found his spot early in life. He was still in his teens when he came across Eagle Island on one of his many camping trips. He fell in love with its rough beauty. After he finished college, he learned that the island was for sale and quite cheap. He bought it with earnings from his first job.

He built a small house on a bare ledge. He wanted it to look like the pilot house of a ship, and it did. The house had only two rooms downstairs. A stone fireplace heated both rooms. There was one small room upstairs. The house did not have a kitchen. In the early years meals were taken at a nearby caretaker's cottage.

Beginning in 1904, Mrs. Peary, daughter Marie, and son Robert, Jr., spent every summer at Eagle Island. Commander Peary joined them when he could. But he was usually in the Arctic. The family came as early as they could in the spring. Sometimes they stayed until late October. The island had plenty of wood for fireplaces and cook stoves. Marie and Robert would have been happy to spend the entire year on Eagle Island.

On September 6, 1909, Josephine Peary and the children were at Eagle Island. It was a lovely, quiet autumn day. Two boats were seen coming toward the island.

The first one tied up at the dock. A man got out and rushed up to the house. He was a newspaper reporter, and he was very excited.

"Your husband has reached the North Pole," he shouted.

Mrs. Peary stayed calm. She had gone through many false alarms. Then the second boat dropped anchor. Out climbed Mr. Palmer, who kept the local store and post office.

Mr. Palmer brought a telegram from Peary himself. It said, "Have made it at last."

It was a great day for Josephine Peary and Marie and Robert, Jr. And for the United States.

Peary retired from the navy in 1911. Small additions had been made to the Eagle Island house over the years. But now Peary had time to fix it up as he had dreamed about for so long.

An army of skilled workmen came to the island. First, they cut two rooms from the house and moved them into the woods. There the rooms were turned into a guest house. Next the house was raised four feet and put on a concrete foundation. Downstairs the workmen built a large dining room, kitchen, maid's room, and bathroom. Upstairs the roof was raised to make room for five bedrooms.

Peary collected three kinds of stones on the island. He had his workmen use them to build a three-sided fireplace. Each side had a different kind of stone. The work crew glassed in porches. The family could now sit and enjoy the view of the sea.

Years later, after Peary died, the family still spent summers on Eagle Island. Then Josephine Peary died in 1955. Her children and grandchildren decided to give Eagle Island to the people of Maine. Now many families can enjoy the Peary's treasured hideaway.

Chapter 9

Honors

The Cook scandal was settled during Peary's lifetime. Yet it is still important to know that since 1911, seven groups have closely studied Peary's claim to have been the first to reach the North Pole. They went over every page of the records he had kept so carefully. They were able to erase all doubt about who was the first man to reach the North Pole. Some of these groups have been:

- Naval Affairs Committee, U.S. House of Representatives
- National Geographical Society
- Royal Geographic Society of London
- The Coast and Geodetic Survey
- Foundation for the Promotion of the Art

of Navigation

These investigations have helped the rest of the world to accept Robert Peary's account of his journey to the Pole. In recent years, new investigations using the latest technology have also reached the same conclusion.

Once Cook's claims had been shown to be false, honors came to Peary thick and fast. He was a proud man so he enjoyed the fame and glory he had brought to his family and his country. Some of his honors and duties included:

- The navy retired him with the rank of rear admiral.
- He was elected president of the American Geographical Society for five years.
- He was selected as a delegate to the International Polar Commission in Rome.
- During World War I he was appointed chairman of the National Aerial Patrol Commission for his support of air power.

- The United States Congress finally and formally recognized his achievements.
- He was given high honors from scientific societies all over the world.
- A chunk of land was named for him. Peary Land is in northern Greenland. It extends about 200 miles east and west along the Arctic Ocean. It is Greenland's largest ice-free area. Peary explored it in 1892, 1895, and 1900.

In his last years, Peary lived a quiet life on Eagle Island. He spent a great deal of time writing. His books include:

- *Secrets of Polar Travel*
- *Snowland Folk*
- *Northward over the Great Ice*
- *The North Pole*

Matthew Henson was not forgotten. In 1913 President Taft saw to it that he was given a good job in the U.S. Customs House in New York City. He received the Congressional Medal from the Congress of the United States honoring him for his part in the North Pole expedition.

Henson wrote his own book about his years with Peary. It was called *A Black Explorer at the North Pole*.

Henson outlived Peary by 35 years. Many years after his death he was reburied in Arlington National Cemetery in Virginia with full honors. That seems fitting and proper since Robert Peary is buried there, too.

A monument made of white Maine granite has been erected at Peary's gravesite. On the monument is a globe with a three-inch bronze star. The star is placed so that it points to the North Pole.